Open Leaves

Harryette Mullen

Published by Black Sunflowers Poetry Press 2023,
www.blacksunflowerspoetry.com

978-1-7396267-1-6

London

Acknowledgments

I thank the editors of *Bayou Magazine*, *Common Ground Review*, *Paperbark*, *Prairie Schooner*, *Terrain*, and *Transition*, where pieces of this work appeared previously.

I am grateful for the shared creative energy of generous friends and family members.

Thanks also to Tiffanie Delune, and especially Amanda Holiday, who made this book a reality.

In memory of
      Miriam Shihab
            Rosemary Catacalos
                Madison Nye

Nothing ends
every blade of grass
remembering your sound

...

let us be one with
the earth expelling anger
spirit unbroken.

— *Sonia Sanchez*

On Land

> What port awaits us?
> — *Robert Hayden*

Onboard, looking out, there is only water for the eye, as far as any eye can see for miles and miles, from here to horizon, today to tomorrow, on and on, for days, weeks, months on end. Thought of land left behind, your name lost at sea, memory set adrift on restless water, vast and endless, though visions of islands delude mind and eye. For now, there is no land, but a world under water too deep to dream, too far to see unless, until you sleep below. The old land all too distant, the land to come so far it might as well be never. Unless, until you survive this passage. Unless, until you live so long you can't believe your eyes or trust your legs to stand upright. Have faith your feet will touch the ground again to walk on land.

Succulents slake their
thirst in intermittent rain-
falls between dry spells.

Organic garden,
a border of marigolds
to repel insects.

Redheaded rooster,
cock's crown, bold celosia's
lush regalia.

Maize that natively
dresses delightfully—not
ever uniform.

Cotton buds to clear
deer's ears, alerted to hear
willow's soft whispers.

Indigenous crop
the Inca cultivated,
Peruvian spud.

Borrow a cup of
utterly yellow luster
from sunshine meadow.

Fine royal garment
fashioned for a butterfly's
fragile dominion.

Mint spreads eagerly.
New roots sprout wherever stems
bow down to touch ground.

Looking up at an
endlessly attentive sky,
yards of blue-eyed grass.

Tousled goldenrod's
invasive weeds, prolific
blonds, butterflies, bees.

The leaves of certain
plants are more ostentatious
than many flowers.

Flourishing natives,
purple Chinese houses bloom
along the highway.

Rose is before a
poet composes or knows
yet what a rose is.

Ink-drenched orchid, your
pink heart swaddled in a black
cloak of mystery.

Cultivate essence
to press or hang in sun to
dry your bluish name.

Chasing Dirt

Nothing will last but trouble and dirt.
— *folk song*

It bounces off me and sticks to you.
— *oral tradition*

Whatever is the matter has lost its place. It can't belong here, but where? Some other place, disordered. That somewhere elsewhere, undone. Wherever the matter comes from. Some place full of space that isn't empty. Entropic creation coughing up dust of burnt-out stars. Too much infinity for vacuum or duster. Too late to filter impure particles. Impossible to remove indelible stains. What would make a space clean and free? What implements, what elements, what solutions? What if we scrub our launch and never find the protoplasmic slime that rhymes with grime? What is the matter breaking down constantly? Dust ball rolling downhill, gathering stray hairs, nail snippets, flakes of sloughed skin. Bits of flying fur with feathers unfurled. To sweep, to be swept, to be moved from place to place, stirred up only to settle again. No way to stay clean when we go chasing dirt. Whatever comes next can eat our dust.

Evergreen scent of
rosemary infuses plain
air with hints of pine.

Asparagus aims
shoots vertically, quiver
of slender arrows.

Let a tomato
tempt you. Be ready to swoon
when ripeness woos you.

Unencumbered vines,
green submarines and rambling
carefree curlicues.

Bright hummingbird sips
hibiscus liquor, fuel
of faithful flower.

Tender flock of lamb's
ears intently listening
for wolf's baneful moan.

Pick, nick—quick. Finish
ambrosial pawpaw's flesh.
Don't bite skin or seeds.

Find frogs and toads in
every yard. No garden is
complete without them.

Tableau of long-stemmed
dancers assembled *en pointe*
in supple tutus.

Every flower a
reminder of all that we
miss when not looking.

A big bucket of
ladybugs, no bargain when
all are free to go.

Open leaves fold, as
if in prayer, offering
a silent blessing.

Glowing lanterns hang
on flaring branches, lemon
illumination.

Not to be confused
with cilantro, as garnish
it isn't paltry.

Loose lettuce leaves a-
head of spring's end. Keep it cool
or lettuce will bolt.

Exploring dark earth,
taproots reaching for sweetness
discover pay dirt.

Flung from Dust

Last year the nation suffered a drought
of unparalleled intensity.
— *Franklin D. Roosevelt*

They believed the land where they settled was theirs for the taking—
so they took it, cleared it, plowed and planted it. Early, before every
spring, they ordered seeds. They turned the soil and prayed for the
right combination of sun and rain.

Each year they trusted that their fields would flourish, that they would
harvest food to survive another winter, that they might live another
year to sow a new crop in the land they had taken, a land that gave and
gave, year after year.

After only a few generations of taking with no thought of giving back,
they saw what had been living soil used up, worn out, left barren.

Still, they plowed furrows into famished earth, hoping that rain
would follow the plow. There had been rainfall; then came years
of deadly drought. No seed would take root in their exhausted
fields. Nothing could grow in lifeless topsoil—no more than a thin
layer of dust, particles of inert matter, with nothing to stop the
wind from picking it up and blowing it from here to yonder across
the plains.

Reckless wind carried dust for miles, covering everything: hunched
bodies leaning against it, lost in chafing blizzards; cars and tractors
buried under suffocating drifts.

The wind swept up the stifling dust and shoved it down their parched throats. They wrapped their faces with shawls and bandanas to keep from swallowing grit that stung their eyes, scratched the sky and darkened midday sun, disastrous as a plague of locusts, a cloud of approaching doom.

At last, to escape devouring wind, they abandoned their vacant fields. Dreaming the abundance of green pastures, they left their homesteads shrouded in worthless dirt. Like dust, flung by wind, like swarming grasshoppers, they picked up and set down in another place. Thinking only of their hunger, and a chance to begin again.

Wind licks a finger,
peeling off flimsy corners,
skimming leafing trees.

Western pygmy blue
butterfly's range expands as
Russian thistle rolls.

Lovers of clover
plant green stuff all over
as forage and cover.

After performing
athletic feats, grasshopper
resting on a leaf.

Of all edible
ovaries, what could taste as
luscious as sweet figs?

Technically a
berry, eggplant flowers, fruits
pale white to purple.

A castle turret
defending the treasury,
protecting the crown.

Though. heartless, never-
theless, stern onion weeps
for poor human creature.

Hedera helix—
climbing tower walls in no
time she grasps it all.

Pink's plentiful when
hills and mountains sing
their farewell to spring.

Kneeling gardener
taking care to consider
the lives of lilies.

Specializing in
digestion, an earthworm is
almost only gut.

Broad sword, crosscut saw,
serrated knife, shark's toothy
jaw, spiked agave.

Canyon sparkles with
water-saving domestic
manzanita scrub.

Copa de oro,
brilliant trophy, on display
in pronghorn valley.

Frequent flyers help
pollinate desert flowers:
bees, bats, white-winged doves.

Exiting Earth

If people were super-optimistic about technology there would be
no reason to be pessimistic about the future.
— *Peter Thiel*

We need to secure the future of consciousness by being
a multi-planet species.
— *Elon Musk*

Life's too short to hang out with people who aren't resourceful.
— *Jeff Bezos*

Money is for making things happen.
— *Richard Branson*

We'll need a spare planet when our sun burns out. This big ball of energy can't go on forever. No such thing as eternal sunshine. It might take billions of years, but the sun will self-destruct, obliterating Earth.

As that event approaches—or sooner, at this rate, if we go on trashing the planet—we'll need an exit strategy. We'd better plan ahead. If we wait too late, our window closes. To be ready, we must prepare for the inevitable end of life as we've known it. Not necessarily ultimate extinction. It's up to us to alter destiny and salvage the future.

The sun collapses, but we carry our unique brilliance to far frontiers of the vaster universe, expanding the electromagnetic field of consciousness into infinity. Projecting the future clarifies the present, as crisis opens opportunities to upgrade the human prototype, exploiting unrealized potential.

Envisioning chaos, determined to survive and profit in unexplored realms of possibility, we invest in smart technological solutions to existential catastrophe. For the sake of prospective humanity in whatever form will evolve, we dedicate ample resources to conquer the unknown and devise an escape before Earth becomes unviable.

Now that we control evolution, the forward path of progress leads to the convergence of organic and inorganic circuits in our reconfigured humanity, as we engineer entities fit for survival in a colonized space of beyond. We choose to evolve to exist in unfamiliar worlds, a challenge we accept. To thrust ourselves off of Earth and shoot into the void, flashing comets trailing cosmic dust.

It's time for sacrifice now to win that distant future. So much of value exists beyond the horizon. If we think long-term, human suffering at this moment may be a prudent down payment for eventual returns. From the point of view of the universe, all of history is a blip, but we set sail, intending to be winners.

We choose to outsource ourselves to a far-off galaxy. No matter, never mind that already the dark edge of infinity beyond blue sky is littered with disposable machines that eventually fall out of orbit, hurled back to Earth.

Gastropods, snails and
slugs, will drown themselves in beer
poured out to entrap.

Firmly planted here
we go digging turnip greens,
uncovering roots.

Okra's baby fuzz
stiffens to bristles; loaded
missiles point to sky.

Zipped tight in their sleep-
ing bags—who could imagine
their deep black-eyed dreams?

Piquant peppers please
taunt tease with tongue-piercing
taste, igniting desire.

Watermelon crossed
Atlantic's perilous waves
with blackseed cargo.

Injuries sustained
while picking berries: snagged skin,
bruised fruit, hurt feelings.

As if a sunburned
sunflower would turn away
from the blazing sun.

Zucchini blossom
nestling under tangled shade,
summing up summer.

Purple clouds gathered
in a brainstorm—artist dreams
of cauliflower.

Harvest moon's fullness,
gravity's captive balloon,
tethered earthbound fruit.

Pungent burning leaves
make sacred smoke, sage's wisps
of healing wisdom.

Indelible juice,
no color seeps deeper than
beet's bleeding red stain.

Walking into it,
full breath of eucalyptus,
this rainy morning.

No one could miss your
strong design, 'til your sleek form
is seen no longer.

Petals so haunting
I'll always remember your
moody blue beauty.

From the Soil

> What would life be without
> homegrown tomatoes?
> ...When I die, don't bury me
> in a box in a cold dark cemetery.
> Out in the garden would be much better,
> 'cause I could be pushing up
> homegrown tomatoes.
>
> — *Guy Clark*

A wild patch of mint surrounding a heap of black soil is all that remains of fitful attempts to cultivate her urban garden. She has given up the effort, content to buy fresh produce at a weekly farmers' market. Her habit of composting kitchen scraps has left her with this mound of rich soil, no longer devoted to growing her own cucumbers, heirloom tomatoes, lettuce, and herbs. Too busy, too distracted, too tired to continue, she has broken a family tradition, moved a further step away from working the soil.

She sees her mother kneeling in her abundant garden, head bowed, as when she plans her planting, consulting the annual *Farmer's Almanac* and leafing through her stack of *Organic Gardening* magazines. Her mother wears faded jeans, a red plaid shirt with a blue paisley bandana around her neck—her face protected from the sun's rays by a wide-brimmed hat of woven sweetgrass. As she kneels on black soil her hands, in green gloves, pluck tender okra pods from their stems and place them in a basket with ripe red tomatoes, just off the vine. She can taste the gumbo, feel on her teeth and tongue the texture of okra.

Her grandfather had a garden. She recalls a picture of him, taken with her grandmother's Brownie camera. He's gripping a pitchfork, turning soil in the yard behind their vernacular bungalow, shirtless in denim overalls, flashing a smile under his sweat-stained straw cowboy hat. At sixteen, he and his mother had a bitter falling out when he told her he was leaving home to go to college. Everyone needed to pitch in, she insisted. To hold on to the family farm and work a living out of it, all the children had to do their part. He was the only one, of all the siblings, to go so far in school.

Somehow, after he'd left, and his father had died, his mother held on to their acres, even during the Great Depression, and beyond. "She was a plain-looking woman, someone who looked like she'd worked hard all her life." Her mother remembers visiting, eating double-yolk eggs from free-range hens, and nearly falling off the back of a skittish horse. Great-grandmother owned that land until her death, when remaining relatives sold the farm and moved to the city. The property they sold is now part of a wealthy suburb, but in the years before her grandfather was born, it was unincorporated land that children of sharecroppers could buy, investing sweat and hope along with their savings.

Her grandmother was a city girl from back east, whose thrifty parents bought what had been a boarding house, the narrow two-story home where their children were born, but her grandfather grew up on his family's farm. His grandparents had been slaves and then sharecroppers. Their children worked for city people, as cooks and washer women, as blacksmiths, porters, and day laborers, striving and saving to buy a piece of land and escape from the city. No need to sweat in Miss Ann's kitchen or Mr. Charlie's blacksmith shop. "Lord knows, I don't want my child to be a white man's yard dog." Soon as they'd earned enough, they bought their own land and built the house on the family farm where her grandfather was born.

By the time he was sixteen, he knew he didn't want to be a farmer. He wanted to study for the ministry. The grandfather of her childhood was the pastor of a church, who wore a black suit with a starched white shirt and dark tie when he stood in the pulpit on Sundays, nodding at her grandmother, who sat at the upright piano. Other days, he sat at a rolltop wooden desk to write his weekly sermons, mixing Bible stories with quotations from his books of history and philosophy.

He listened to country western music on the radio. He liked to go fishing. He enjoyed working in the household garden, growing leafy greens, tomatoes, okra, watermelon, and black-eyed peas. He took pleasure in eating fresh food, homegrown. It wasn't the same as being a farmer, pulling a living from the soil. Her mother remembers family meals with cousins, aunts, and uncles—occasions for telling jokes and stories. "When Pop got together with his relatives, they could make a mule laugh out loud." Gardens sprouted under their hands as they moved to houses in the city, starting new plots.

"You won't starve if you can grow your own food. If you take care of your green patch, it will take care of you." Growing up, she helped her mother in the family garden. She fed and watered earthworms they raised in a worm farm, a bin filled with dark soil tunneled by pinkish worms, kept in a shady spot and sprinkled daily. Expert composters, worms thrive with scraps and peels of fruits and vegetables, eggshells, coffee grounds, and moist soil. Their castings—worm poop—fertilize the garden, turning earth into black gold.

Her grandfather would pay her to dig her fingers into their bed and extract worms from the soil, a nickel each. He used them as bait when he went fishing. "The worms don't bite, but they get the fish to bite." She overcame her squeamishness enough to handle the cool, wet wigglers, but could not bring herself to bait a fish hook with a live worm. Yet, she never objected to the catch of the day that landed on her dinner plate with a garden salad. When she scoops a handful of black earth, she thinks of living things that keep the soil alive.

Harryette Mullen's books include *Recyclopedia* (Graywolf, 2006), winner of a PEN Beyond Margins Award, and *Sleeping with the Dictionary* (University of California, 2002), a finalist for a National Book Award, National Book Critics Circle Award, and Los Angeles Times Book Prize. A collection of essays and interviews, *The Cracks Between What We Are and What We Are Supposed to Be* (University of Alabama, 2012) won an Elizabeth Agee Prize. Graywolf published *Urban Tumbleweed: Notes from a Tanka Diary* in 2013. *Her Silver-Tongued Companion*, a critical edition of her poetry, is forthcoming from Edinburgh University.

Tiffanie Delune image credits

www.blacksunflowerspoetry.com